CADILLAC
CLASSICS

CADILLAC

CLASSICS

BY THE AUTO EDITORS OF CONSUMER GUIDE®

Publications International, Ltd.

Louis Weber, CEO
Publications International, Ltd.
7373 North Cicero Avenue
Lincolnwood, Illinois 60712

Permission is never granted for commercial purposes.

ISBN-13: 978-1-4127-1534-8
ISBN-10: 1-4127-1534-2

Manufactured in China.

8 7 6 5 4 3 2 1

Library of Congress Control Number: 2007932081

Credits

Photography:
The editors would like to thank the following people and organizations for supplying the photography that made this book possible. They are listed below, along with the page number(s) of their photos.

Joe Bohovic: 65; **Scott Brandt:** 27; **Thomas Glatch:** 121; **Sam Griffith:** 61, 71, 93, 99, 113; **John Heilig:** 9, 39; **Don Heiny:** 109; **Bud Juneau:** 13, 17, 31, 35, 47, 59, 91; **Milton Kieft:** 83; **Vince Manocchi:** 21, 23, 43, 49, 67, 79, 101, 127, 128; **Doug Mitchel:** 53, 55, 63, 85, 87, 97, 105; **Mike Mueller:** 69, 95; **David Newhardt:** 15, 25; **Nina Padgett:** 41, 73, 75; **Jay Peck:** 89; **Rob Reaser:** 77; **David Temple:** 57; **Phil Toy:** 123; **W.C. Waymack:** 37, 45, 103, 115; 117; **Nicky Wright:** 11, 19, 81, 107, 111, 125

Back Cover: Sam Griffith; Vince Manocchi; Nina Padgett

Special thanks to: Kenneth F. Ruddock/Ken's Memory Lane

Owners:
Special thanks to the owners of the cars featured in this book for their cooperation. Their names and the page number(s) for their vehicles follow.

AACA Museum: 9; **David Aiken:** 109; **Daniel Allen:** 29; **Gary Bacon:** 77; **The Blackhawk Collection:** 41, back cover; **Peter Bose:** 85, 97, 105; **E.R. Bufkin:** 63; **Nicola Bulgari:** 39; **Cadillac Manufacturing:** 33, 119; **Otis Chandler Vintage Museum:** 25; **John Diefenbach:** 103; **Orville Dopps:** 128; **Bob and Gail Elwood:** 75; **Joseph Falore:** 123; **Robert and Gene Fattore:** 99; **Eugene Fattore, Jr.:** 113; **Fraser Dante Limited:** 89; **Howard V. Funck:** 37; **Ed Gunther:** 47; **Robert P. Hallada:** 91; **Gordon F. Harvey:** 53; **Jack Heacock:** 43; **Bill Henefelt:** 95; **Wally Herman:** 73; **Larry Hills:** 101; **Thomas Hollfelder:** 23; **Owen Hoyt:** 13; **Joe D. James:** 45; **Elliott and Katharine Klein:** 19; **Larry Klein:** 17; **Dr. Gerald M. Levitt:** 65; **Ron Lipsey:** 57; **Warren and Sylvia Louridsen:** 55; **Larry Martin:** 115; **Roy and Bonnie McClain:** 79, back cover; **Ray Menefee:** 59; **Rod Morris:** 69; **National Park Service:** 31; **Tenny Natkin:** 71; **Harry Nicks:** 67, back cover; **Ed Oberhaus:** 81, 107, 111, 125; **John W. Petras:** 93, back cover; **Dick Pyle:** 61; **Ted and Jo Raines:** 35; **Rick Roberts:** 117; **Joseph Rotor:** 51; **Paul Schinnerer:** 15; **Ted Spicuzza:** 121; **Richard Stanley:** 49; **Robert Supalla:** 87; **R. Wayne Turner:** 83; **H. Washburn:** 127; **Fred Weber:** 27; **Western Reserve Historical Society Crawford Collection:** 11

CONTENTS

6

FOREWORD

The one-cylinder Cadillac of 1902 was a far cry from the luxury cars that would make the name famous, but it was built with precision. Cadillac founder Henry Leland was known as the "Master of Precision" because of his obsession with inter-changeable parts. In 1908, three Cadillacs were disassembled, their parts mixed up, then reassembled into three cars that ran perfectly. Cadillac won the prestigious Dewar Trophy for that feat, and it inspired the make's "Standard of the World" slogan. Cadillac moved into the luxury field, and its engineering devel-opments enhanced its reputation. Among Cadillac's firsts were the electric self-starter, production V-8 engine, synchromesh transmission, safety glass, and V-16 engine. Cadillac's innova-tions changed the way we drive. It is hard to imagine a world without V-8s, where one has to crank start engines. Cadillac's 1915 V-8 set standards for smoothness and power. It proved its reliability on the battlefields of World War I. Cadillac gained status in the Thirties with classic styling and V-16 engines. After World War II, Cadillac's overhead-valve V-8 set the pace for American powerplants. Its tailfin styling was copied around the world. Cadillac became the symbol of success. During the prosperity of the Fifties and Sixties Cadillac built the big, com-fortable cars that Americans aspired to own. The Seventies were a difficult time, but Cadillac had success with its "international size" Seville. Through it all, Cadillac published wonderful ads. The Thirties featured elegant drawings of fashionable people, while ads from the Fifties were graced by jewelry from top jewelers, along with elegant women's clothes and furs. In the Sixties, drawings gave way to skilled photography. This book brings together the advertising and the cars of Cadillac.

1912
MODEL THIRTY

Cadillac introduced the first electric self-starter on its 1912 cars. Prior to the self-starter, cars were started by hand cranking—a task that was not only strenuous but sometimes dangerous. Thanks to the self-starter, driving was safer and no longer restricted to the strong. In 1913 Cadillac won its second Dewar Trophy for the self-starter. Cadillac won its first Dewar in 1908 for the precision of its interchangeable parts. The trophy was presented by the Royal Automobile Club of England and was quite prestigious. Cadillac considered the award justification for its "Standard of the World" slogan. The Model Thirty was powered by 33-hp 4-cylinder engine and good for about 50 mph. The car was well made with good materials such as copper for the water jackets. The touring car cost $1800.

1915
TYPE 51

Cadillac leapfrogged its six-cylinder challengers in the luxury car field by jumping from a four cylinder to the world's first mass production V-8. Cadillac developed the V-8 under tight security and surprised the competition. The V-8 engine had the advantage of being more compact than an in-line six. By the mid-Fifties, the majority of American cars would be powered by a V-8. Cadillac's first V-8 was smooth running, quiet, and reliable. It developed 70 hp from 314 cid. Open cars were capable of 65 mph. Prices ranged from $1975 to $3600. Surprisingly, prices were the same as those on the four-cylinder models of the year before. The seven-passenger touring car pictured cost $2075. The steering wheel pivoted to allow easy entry and exit. Cadillac built 13,000 during the first year of V-8 production.

Comprenez - vous ?...

SHARING FIRST PLACE WITH CADILLAC

When comparisons are suggested between lesser cars and the La Salle, it will pay to remember that the General Motors Corporation—manufacturer of the leading automobiles in every grade—is behind the creation of this especial value in automobiles. The La Salle shares with Cadillac the famous 90-degree, V-type, eight-cylinder engine—together with first place in the fine car field.

FOR A SMALL DOWN PAYMENT—with the appraisal value of your used car acceptable as cash—you may possess a La Salle on the liberal term-payment plan of the General Motors Acceptance Corporation—the famous G.M.A.C. plan.

CADILLAC MOTOR CAR COMPANY
DIVISION OF GENERAL MOTORS CORPORATION
DETROIT, MICHIGAN   OSHAWA, CANADA

LA SALLE
Priced from $2495 to $2685, f. o. b. Detroit

· MANUFACTURED · COMPLETELY · BY · THE · CADILLAC · MOTOR · CAR · COMPANY · WITHIN · ITS · OWN · PLANTS ·

1927
LASALLE SERIES 303

LaSalle was Cadillac's "companion car," built to fill a price gap in General Motors' hierarchy between Buick and Cadillac. The convertible coupe cost $2635—$800 less than the comparable Cadillac. LaSalle was seven inches shorter than the standard Cadillac and was meant to be more of driver's car. Its 75-hp V-8 was a smaller version of the Cadillac engine. Styling was by Harley Earl who created General Motors' Art and Colour Section and influenced the look of GM cars for the next 30 years. La-Salle was his first project, and it was the first car designed by a stylist instead of an engineer. It is appropriate that the ad is set in France because the French-built Hispano-Suisa heavily influenced Earl's design. The '27 LaSalle was a hit and sold more than 10,000 cars in its short introductory model year.

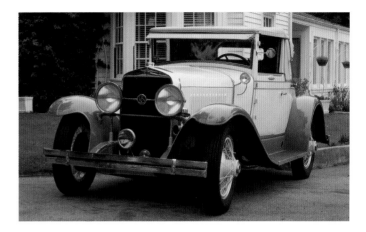

SIXTEEN CYLINDERS

Custom-built . . . the most highly
personalized of all motor cars

CADILLAC MOTOR CAR COMPANY . . . DIVISION OF GENERAL MOTORS

1930
SIXTEEN

The smooth-running V-16 was Cadillac's bid to domi-
nate the American luxury car market. The first production V-16 displaced 452 cid and was rated at 165 hp,
although actual power was probably 200. Either way,
there was enough power to propel a big limousine to
90 mph in silence. Prices for cars with catalog bodies
ranged from $5350 to $9700 at a time when Chevro-
lets started at $495. The $6650 all-weather phaeton
pictured sold 250 copies during 1930–31, while the
Imperial landau cabriolet in the ad sold only two.
Although launched after the stock market crash, the
Sixteen's introduction was a huge success with 3250
sold during 1930–31. That was an impressive number
for a car of that price. For instance, Marmon sold only
223 of its own well-engineered V-16s in '31.

It is really hopeless to try to find its value equal

THERE is no let-down in La Salle from Cadillac standards—instead, a steady measuring up to the highest of manufacturing and decorative ideals . . . ¶ You are not penalized by a "saving" here and a skimping there, because La Salle is very moderately priced . . . ¶ On the contrary, you are profited and benefited by the fact that Cadillac and La Salle with their two great high grade markets utilize *all* of the resources of the vast plants which they jointly occupy . . . ¶ Cadillac saves for La Salle and La Salle for Cadillac, and in quality they both draw from the same rich sources and march hand-in-hand in sharing economies and efficiencies . . . ¶ Perhaps Cadillac has been over conservative in presenting La Salle for two years—preferring to wait until La Salle had proved itself worthy of its Cadillac birthright . . . ¶ The time has come now to point the Cadillac finger of pride at La Salle and to ask you in all sincerity and earnestness to scour the market and satisfy yourself how hopeless it is to try to find La Salle's value equal . . . ¶ Power for power, size for size, acceleration for acceleration, ease for ease, beauty for beauty, price for price—La Salle stands out as distinctly alone in value as Cadillac itself . . . ¶ Cadillac Motor Car Company, Division of General Motors.

La SALLE

COMPANION CAR TO CADILLAC

1930
LASALLE SERIES 340

With the Depression taking hold, this LaSalle ad emphasized value. The difference in price between the $2590 LaSalle convertible coupe and the Cadillac V-8 version represented more than $1000 in savings. Both the convertible coupe (pictured) and the roadster (illustrated in the ad) had rumble seats. Sales of luxury cars were decimated in the early Thirties, and Cadillac needed the extra sales provided by its lower-priced companion make. Appearance of LaSalles and Cadillac was merging as the years progressed since LaSalle's 1927 introduction. Horsepower ratings were also getting closer, with LaSalle's 340-cid V-8 producing 90 hp while Cadillac's 353-cid V-8 put out 95. The heads of both LaSalle and Cadillac V-8s were ribbed to improve cooling and dress up the engine room.

Of all the reasons why the Cadillac V-16 has met with such favor, none is more important than the fact that it permits complete expression of the purchaser's preference as to body style and appointments. Fleetwood has executed more than thirty V-16 body types, each one highly distinctive in its basic design, and available in a variety of finishes and interior fabrics. In addition, special custom creations may be had in any mode the purchaser specifies. Any Cadillac-La Salle dealer will gladly provide complete information.

CADILLAC V $^{8}_{12}$ 16

1931
SIXTEEN

By 1931, Cadillac was building eight-, twelve-, and sixteen-cylinder engines. Prices ranged from $2695 for a V-8 coupe to $9700 for the Sixteen Fleetwood transformable town Brougham shown in the ad. The Madam X Imperial sedan pictured cost $7525. The Madam X name was from a popular play of '29. This right-hand-drive car is believed to have been used by the U.S. embassy in London. Cadillac cataloged a wide array of custom bodies produced in small numbers by Cadillac-owned Fleetwood coachbuilders. A few styles sold several hundred copies, while only one or two bodies were built in other styles. A customer could satisfy almost any whim without leaving the Fleetwood catalog, or he could commission a true one-of-a-kind custom body for even more money.

The Cadillac V-16 Convertible Coupe, illustrated below, seems a standing invitation to take the wheel and drive. This attractive creation is from the custom shops of Fleetwood. Prices of the V-16 range from $5350, f.o.b. Detroit.

Cadillac's introduction of multi-cylinder motoring is one of the greatest and most fundamental advancements for which this organization has ever been responsible. In fact, it has resulted in a complete change in the basic conception of how luxurious a motor car can be. The finest embodiment of the multi-cylinder principle is found in the Cadillac V-16—a car so advanced from every standpoint that only those who have driven it can appreciate how really exceptional it is. Even the veteran fine car owner can look forward to a glorious experience when first he tries a V-16. May we suggest, therefore, that you take this car for an informative demonstration?

CADILLAC V⁸₁₂T6

1931
SIXTEEN

At 5310 lbs, the roadster pictured was the lightest of the V-16 line and could approach 100 mph or cruise at over 70. The convertible coupe in the ad was 300 lbs heavier but could still exceed 90 mph. Cadillac knew that salesmen, as well as proud owners, would raise the hood to show off the 16-cylinder motor and made sure that no one was disappointed. The sight of sixteen cylinders with overhead valves was impressive enough, but the engine was neatly laid out and well balanced. Finished in black enamel, polished aluminum, and chrome, it was an aesthetic triumph. The rear deck of the roadster and convertible had a rumble seat for two additional passengers and an access door for golf club storage. In addition, there was a folding rack on which a trunk could be mounted.

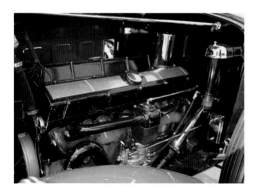

A man and his Motor Car

Of all those material possessions which bespeak a man's place among his fellow men — none is more instantly recognized than his automobile. Wherever he goes and whatever he does, his car has come to be accepted as a symbol of his tastes, his standing and his business success. Because of this, there has grown up about Cadillac and La Salle a degree of respect which is unusual in America's business life. Men who have given the problem serious thought will have no other automobile; for here is the "Standard of the World"— the car which has stood, for thirty years, as the emblem of all that is fine. They know, when they drive a Cadillac or La Salle, that they have the masterpiece itself—and that it is given the recognition which a masterpiece always inspires. La Salle prices from $2395, Cadillac from $2795, f. o. b. Detroit.

CADILLAC

The Cadillac V-12 All Weather Phaeton

22

1932
TWELVE

The V-12, introduced in late 1930, was basically a V-16 with four fewer cylinders. The V-16 displaced 452 cid and developed 165 hp while the V-12 was 368-cid and put out 135 hp. The lighter Twelves used a shorter chassis than the Sixteens and were almost as fast. A roadster could exceed 85 mph. They were also almost as smooth and silent as the V-16s. The All-Weather Phaeton was available on V-8, V-12, and V-16 chassis. As shown on the Twelve chassis, it cost $4195—$1000 less than the Sixteen. The less expensive Twelve took sales from the flagship Sixteen. In '32, 1709 Twelves were built versus only 296 Sixteens. Cadillac's one-two punch with V-16 and V-12 had its effect in breaking Packard's dominance of the luxury car market. Packard built only 549 of its own V-12 in '32.

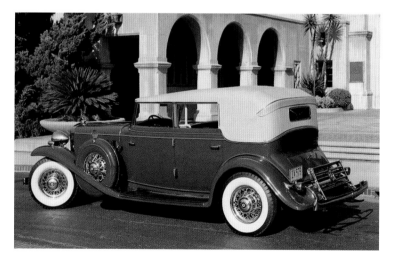

1932
SIXTEEN

Cadillac offered several sedan bodies on the Sixteen chassis. The ad shows a basic 5-passenger sedan. The car pictured is a Fleetwood Madam X 7-passenger sedan built for General Motors Canada president R.S. McLaughlin. The Madam X bodies had a more extreme windshield slant with thinner pillars, among other distinctive features. Beside the usual gauges in the instrument panel was one for "Ride Regulation" that registered the firmness of the adjustable shock absorbers. Mounted around the horn button were switches for the throttle and headlights. The headlights had two ranges of high and low beams—one for country driving and the other for city.

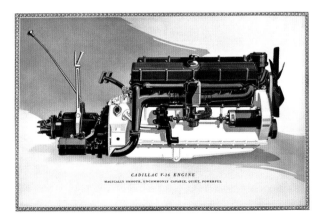

CADILLAC V-16 ENGINE
MAGICALLY SMOOTH, UNCOMMONLY CAPABLE, QUIET, POWERFUL

*You'll always be glad
you selected a*
CADILLAC

It is an interesting and significant fact that men and women are literally loath to part with their Cadillacs. Even when the time has obviously arrived to exchange an old Cadillac for a new one, the owner almost invariably surrenders his car with a feeling of reluctance. And it is quite understandable that such should be the case—for a Cadillac is so delightful to drive, so satisfying to own, and so unfailingly dependable that it becomes wellnigh inseparable from the joy and pleasure of its owner's existence. And never has any Cadillac offered so much to endear it to its owners as do the distinguished new cars which now bear the Cadillac crest. Surpassingly beautiful, exceptionally dynamic in their performance, and luxuriously comfortable—these new creations are undeniably among the finest possessions a man could possibly acquire. In fact, there can be no question that you'll always be glad you selected a Cadillac. Cadillac prices range from $2795, f. o. b. Detroit.

CADILLAC

V 8 12 16

The Cadillac V-8 Sport Phaeton

1932
SIXTEEN

Cadillac bodies were similar for Eights, Twelves, and Sixteens. The main difference between the V-16 sport phaeton pictured and the V-8 sport phaeton shown in the ad is the length of the hood—although the artist has exaggerated the V-8's hood. The V-8 sport phaeton cost $3245 and weighed 4800 lbs, while the V-16 version cost $4945 and weighed 5500 lbs. Cadillac's side-valve V-8 developed 115 hp from 353 cid. The sport phaeton was good for about 85 mph. All models rode on a similar chassis and shared features such as power-assisted brakes and clutch, as well as adjustable shock absorbers. The V-8 owner enjoyed most of the speed and comfort of the multi-cylinder Cadillacs for substantially less money. Only 4698 Cadillacs were built in '32: 2693 V-8s, 1709 V-12s, and 296 V-16s.

The New LaSalle V-8 Convertible Coupe

1932
LASALLE SERIES 345-B

LaSalle and Cadillac shared the same 115-hp V-8, but LaSalle's 130- and 136-inch wheelbases were four inches shorter than the Cadillac Eight's wheelbases. This convertible coupe rode on the 130-inch wheelbase and cost $2545—$400 less than the similar Cadillac model. LaSalle probably had a thinner profit margin, as the main difference between the two brands was trim. The LaSalle's instrument panel was almost identical to Cadillac's and also included a "Ride Regulation" gauge that displayed the setting of the standard adjustable shock absorbers. LaSalle was named for the French explorer who claimed the Louisiana Territory for France. LaSalle was killed by his own men and might not have been the best mascot for a car, but the label was consistent with Cadillac—named for another French explorer who founded Detroit.

IT HAS been for so long an established custom among certain families to own a Cadillac, that many of them buy their cars without particular thought as to their mechanical fitness. And well *may* these staunch Cadillac advocates take for granted the excellence of their cars—for their trust will never be misplaced. Yet, the Cadillac owner who fails to consider his car *mechanically* is denying himself a great deal of satisfaction. . . . After all, a motor car *is* largely mechanical; and its mechanisms are extremely important. It ought, therefore, to be of the utmost reassurance to reflect that Cadillac engineering has set the world a standard for these many years; that Cadillac's limits of precision are so exacting as literally to stagger the imagination; and that its craftsmen have back of them a tradition more binding in its requirements than any actual rules you could possibly formulate. . . . . In fact, it is because of *these* things that Cadillac has come to occupy the unchallenged position it does among America's first families. . . . We suggest, therefore, that when you purchase your next Cadillac you give a thought to mechanics, too. It is certain to increase your satisfaction as a Cadillac owner.

Cadillac list prices begin at $2695, f.o.b. Detroit. Thirty-two Fisher and Fleetwood body types. Convenient G. M. A. C. terms may be utilized.

CADILLAC
A GENERAL MOTORS VALUE

1933
SIXTEEN

Cadillac eased into the streamlined age with skirted fenders and vee'd grilles. The ad shows a town cabriolet with an open chauffeur's compartment. The front compartment could be closed during bad weather. The town cabriolet is mounted on a V-8 or V-12 chassis. The Cadillac Sixteen Imperial cabriolet sedan pictured— the only one of its kind—was originally owned by railway magnate Frederick Vanderbilt. Although the roof over the chauffeur was solid, there was a roll-down glass division between the front and rear compartments. Cadillac announced that 1933 V-16 production would be limited to 400 cars, but only 126 were sold that year. Sales of super luxury cars were falling fast as the Depression reached its peak. The fact that the V-16 averaged eight miles to a gallon didn't help.

LEADERSHIP RESTS ON ACHIEVEMENT

Cadillac WAS FIRST WITH SYNCRO-MESH TRANSMISSION

It was a significant day, indeed, when the Cadillac Motor Car Company announced that it had perfected a non-clashing transmission — one that would enable the driver to shift without reducing his speed, and without noise or grinding of gears! . . . This great advancement, called then and now the Syncro-Mesh Transmission, has resulted in a complete transformation of the act of gear-shifting — and made motoring infinitely safer and more enjoyable. . . . The same spirit of pioneering which enabled Cadillac to produce the Syncro-Mesh Transmission is kept endlessly alive in the Cadillac laboratories, and is evident everywhere in the new Cadillacs and La Salles. In fact, among many other advancements, these new cars reveal an improvement in the transmission itself, for the Cadillac-La Salle Syncro-Mesh is now silent in operation in all forward speeds — low, second and high. . . . This constant pioneering has caused many persons to hold to Cadillac and La Salle during year after year without so much as considering the purchase of other cars — for they know that every practical advancement will be given them in these two distinguished creations. . . . Your Cadillac-La Salle dealer will gladly acquaint you with today's Cadillacs and La Salles — now, as always, foremost examples of the finest automotive craftsmanship. La Salle list prices start at $2245, Cadillac at $2695, f. o. b. Detroit.

The Syncro-Mesh Transmission, one of the great developments in the history of the automobile, was introduced by Cadillac in August, 1928. It was, and is, a marked example of Cadillac's leadership in the fundamental advancement of the motor car

MAGELLAN, FIRST TO CIRCUMNAVIGATE THE GLOBE

THE CADILLAC V-12 ALL-WEATHER PHAETON

1933
EIGHT

Although known as a maker of luxury cars, Cadillac made a contribution to performance driving with the introduction of the synchromesh transmission on its 1929 model cars. Prior to synchromesh, drivers had to pause during each shift and match engine speed to road speed before releasing the clutch. Synchromesh made shifting faster and much easier. It is still used in every manual transmission today. An innovation shared with other General Motors' cars in '33 was "No-Draft Ventilation." Pivoting vent panes were incorporated in the front and rear side windows to regulate the flow of air to the interior. Window vents were common on cars until air conditioning gained popularity in the Sixties. A V-12 all-weather phaeton is shown in the ad, while the car pictured is a V-8 sedan.

LA SALLE CONVERTIBLE COUPE

A FINER AND FAR MORE DISTINGUISHED LA SALLE
... at an even more moderate price

It was an occasion for great rejoicing among men and women who admire fine possessions, when the new La Salle V-Eight appeared upon the American scene a few weeks ago. For here was something they had been seeking. Here was a motor car of proud lineage, enriched throughout in its quality—yet offered at prices in perfect keeping with the current economic scheme. No need to question the correctness of the youthful grace which is the dominating note in its appearance—for the style of the new La Salle was created by the most accomplished designers at the command of the Fisher studios. No need to wonder about its mechanical fitness or the nature of its performance—for La Salle is the product of the same skilled craftsmen who build those magnificent motor cars, the Cadillac V-Eight, V-Twelve, and V-Sixteen. The new La Salle is powered by the 115-horsepower Cadillac V-type eight-cylinder engine. Throughout chassis and body are many refinements and developments of major importance, including the new Fisher No-Draft Ventilation system, individually-controlled. Yet the standard five-passenger sedan is now reduced to $2245, f.o.b. Detroit —a price most attractively reasonable for a car of Cadillac design, Cadillac construction, and genuine Cadillac quality.

LA SALLE V·8
A General Motors Value

1933
LASALLE SERIES 345-C

In the worst year of the Depression, LaSalle's production was up slightly from 3386 in '32 to 3482. Many of LaSalle's sales were at the expense of Cadillac, where production slipped from 4698 to 3983. Although the streamlined styling was new for '33, the chassis and 115-hp V-8 engine were carried over from the previous year. LaSalle's original mission was to not only plug a price gap between Cadillac and Buick, but also to build a smaller, sportier car. By 1930, LaSalles were almost as big as Cadillac V-8s and almost identical in styling and engineering. LaSalle was a cheaper Cadillac but built and finished to the same high standard. The coupe pictured was LaSalle's lowest priced car at $2245. The sidemounted spare tires were optional. The convertible coupe in the ad cost $2395.

1934
EIGHT

Cadillacs rode more comfortably in '34 thanks to new independent front suspension that replaced the former beam axle. Horsepower for the V-8 rose from 115 to 130. New styling included pontoon-shaped fenders and bumpers inspired by biplanes. The bumpers were spring loaded to retract during low-speed impacts. Unfortunately, the bumpers were as delicate as they looked and expensive to repair. They were replaced by conventional bumpers after only one year. The car in the ad is an Imperial convertible sedan. "Imperial" was Cadillac's term for cars with divider windows between front and back seats. In this convertible sedan, the divider would have provided the rear passenger some protection against wind with top down. The car pictured is a five-passenger town sedan.

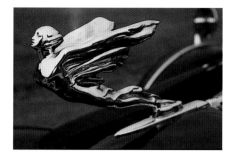

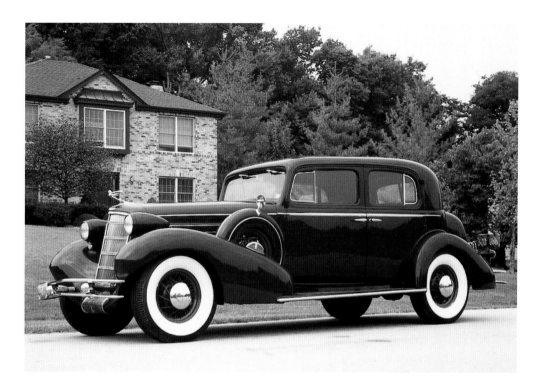

1934
LASALLE SERIES 350

LaSalles were too expensive to sell well during the Depression, but as detrimmed Cadillacs they couldn't be sold for much less. The solution was to design a new '34 LaSalle using Oldsmobile components. The 95-hp straight eight was based on the Olds engine but was assembled in the Cadillac plant and benefited from upgrades such as aluminum pistons and a high compression head. LaSalle used Olds' 119-inch chassis with independent front suspension. The styling was uniquely LaSalle. Legend has it that General Motors planned to kill LaSalle after '33, but Harley Earl unveiled a full-size mock-up for GM management who were so bowled over by the long-hooded beauty that LaSalle was saved. LaSalle started at $1495—which was more than $1000 lower than the cheapest Cadillac.

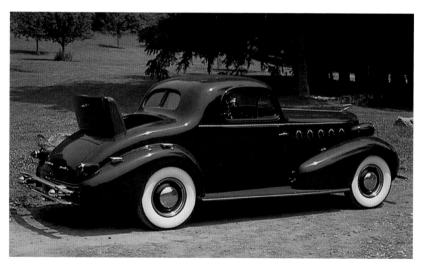

Cadillac-Fleetwood
TOWN CABRIOLET

Cadillac-Fleetwood Town Cabriolet, $4445

Never in the history of the motor car industry has there been another name with the significance of Cadillac-Fleetwood. Everywhere, it has come to connote the highest attainment in the motor car builder's art—chassis by Cadillac, body by Fleetwood. For the new Cadillac chassis, Fleetwood has designed and fashioned the finest coachcraft it has ever produced. Beautiful, completely luxurious in every detail of fitment and finish, and highly individual in both appearance and form—the new Fleetwood creations stand unique and alone in every aspect of their excellence. Fleetwood builds bodies for the Cadillac Eight, Twelve and Sixteen. The car shown above is the Eight-cylinder Cadillac chassis and the body is the Fleetwood Town Cabriolet. This body is also available on the Twelve-cylinder Cadillac chassis.

KNEE-ACTION • HYDRAULIC BRAKES • CENTER-POINT STEERING • TURRET-TOP
TWO RIDE STABILIZERS • PEAK-LOAD GENERATOR • TRIPLE-RANGE CHOKE

THE *Spearhead*
OF MOTORING PROGRESS

Surely it is not assuming too much to suggest that all cars are better cars today as a result of the high standards established by Cadillac thirty years ago and progressively maintained ever since. • • Motorists generally have always recognized, and even required, that Cadillac should give unmistakable evidence of its right to a distinct leadership in engineering, in handling, in riding, and in luxury. • • Yet much as all cars have improved as a result of example and public requirement, Cadillac in the Royal Family of Motordom has held fast and even emphasized these distinguished differences. • • It is a pleasant thing that Cadillac attains the peak of its thirty years of achievement at the same time that it records the lowest prices in more than two decades. • • If you are disposed to question the almost universal admission that Cadillac's cars surpass others in riding and driving, in comfort and in beauty—that Cadillac is still the spearhead of motoring progress—the briefest demonstration will reassure you. • • Cadillac has never done as well by its public in performance, in appearance, in value, as in the current cars.

EVIDENCE OF CADILLAC LEADERSHIP

First to adopt Standardized Parts and make them interchangeable • • First to employ the famous Johansson Gauges • • First to equip cars with Electric Starting, Lighting and Ignition • • First to offer Closed Bodies as standard • • First to build V-type, Eight-cylinder Engines • • First to develop Thermostatic Control of the cooling system • • First to completely protect its owners with Security Plate Glass • • First to perfect the clashless Syncro-Mesh Transmission • • First to build a 16-cylinder Automobile Engine • • First to introduce Crankcase Ventilation • • First to use Hydraulic Valve Silencers • • First to develop Knee-Action • • First to establish Country Wide Service on a uniform basis.

Prices list at Detroit, subject to change without notice. Special equipment extra. Offered on G.M.A.C.'s new 6% Time Payment Plan. A General Motors Value.

La Salle $1175   *Cadillac* $1645

CADILLAC
Fleetwood $2445

THE ROYAL FAMILY OF MOTORDOM

1936
SERIES 90 FLEETWOOD

Cadillac named its V-16 line the Series 90 Fleetwood for '36 and built only 52. Only one wore the town cabriolet body pictured, which cost $8850. The car in the ad has a similar town cabriolet body mounted on a V-8 chassis that, at $4445, cost about half as much. The V-16's hp had risen to 185 in 1934, the same year its wheelbase increased to a lengthy 154 inches. All Cadillacs gained hydraulic brakes in '36. Previously, Cadillac used power-assisted mechanical brakes. The '36 V-16s got General Motors' all-steel "Turret Top" a year later than V-8s. Early closed cars used a roof panel of treated fabric that sometimes leaked and had to be dressed every few years. GM claimed its new turret top was safer as well as maintenance-free. Among the Cadillac firsts listed in the ad were: interchangeable parts, electric starting, production V-8 and V-16 engines, safety glass, and synchromesh transmission.

1936
SERIES 60

The new Series 60 line was substantially cheaper than previous Cadillacs. The touring sedan pictured cost $1695. The least expensive '35 Cadillac had cost $2345. Cadillac kept Series 60 production costs down with a shorter 121-inch wheelbase and a body shell shared with Buick. Also reducing costs was a new, simpler-to-build V-8. The new V-8 displaced 322 cid and deveoped 125 hp in the Series 60. In larger Cadillacs, the V-8 was 346 cid with 135 hp. The 150-hp V-12 was in its next-to-last year of production. The Series 80 Fleetwood touring sedan in the ad was powered by the V-12 and cost $3145. It looks remarkably similar to the less expensive Series 60. Production more than tripled, and Cadillac built 12,880 cars in '36. Almost half of those were Series 60s.

CADILLAC SHOWS THE WORLD!

Only four years ago
a Cadillac cost *twice as much*
$1555* AND UP

A General Motors Value

If you are accustomed to think of a Cadillac as a car beyond your reach, simply remember the new Cadillac price. It is $1555*—*the lowest Cadillac price in twenty-eight years!*

Yet the Cadillac of today is built to the same high standards so evident in every Cadillac of the past. The new Series 60 Cadillac is even larger, even finer and more powerful than before.

When you drive the new Cadillac, its performance will hold you spellbound. This 135-horsepower V-8 responds as no car ever responded before—so smoothly, so quietly, and with such exhilarating power that you will never again be satisfied with anything short of a Cadillac.

Visit your Cadillac dealer. Let the new Cadillac speak for itself. Its economy will come as a most agreeable surprise. Its beauty and luxury will be all that you expect —and more. Its completeness from every standpoint will convince you that Cadillac leads in *value* as it does in *quality.*

*Delivered price at Detroit, Mich., $1555 and up, subject to change without notice. This price includes all standard accessories. Transportation, State and Local Sales Taxes, Optional Accessories and Equipment—Extra. Model illustrated is equipped with white sidewall tires and wheel discs at extra cost.

FROM THE ROYAL FAMILY OF MOTORDOM

1937
SERIES 60

Cadillac's successful Series 60 was bigger and more powerful for its second year. Wheelbase increased from 121 inches to 124, while the 125-hp V-8 was replaced by a larger 135-hp V-8. The convertible sedan pictured was new to the Series 60 line and, at $2120, was the most expensive. The $1555 2-passenger coupe in the ad was the cheapest. The Series 60 was considerably less expensive than other Cadillac models and took the make into a lower price range. However, the ad was a little loose with math when it said "Only four years ago a Cadillac cost twice as much." For that to have been true, the cheapest '33 Cadillac would have cost $3110, but an Eight 2-passenger coupe was only $2695. Cadillac built 14,152 cars in '37 of which 7000 were Series 60s.

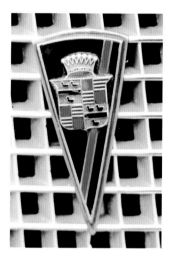

Look at LaSalle! *V-8*

LaSalle IS ECONOMICAL ALL ALONG THE LINE!

Low price is but a *part* of the economy of motor car ownership. The cost of service and operation are of equal importance.

Fortunately, when you buy a LaSalle V-8, you can be certain of economy *all along the line!* For LaSalle is not only easy to *buy*—but it is also inexpensive to *own* and *operate!*

LaSalle, you know, is built by Cadillac. It has Cadillac engineering and construction. Consequently, LaSalle does not need the servicing generally required by motor cars. It does not reveal the usual wear and tear as the miles

pile up. Furthermore, a LaSalle V-8 runs a surprising distance on a gallon of gasoline. And *no* car is more sparing in its use of oil.

In fact, all things considered, you can own a LaSalle for about as little as any car you could buy. And, of course, LaSalle will give you *much more* than any car below it in price.

Why not LOOK AT LaSALLE today?

*Delivered price Detroit, $1095 and up, subject to change without notice. Model shown: Five-Passenger Touring Sedan—$1260. Prices include all standard accessories. Transportation, State and Local Sales Taxes, Optional Accessories and Equipment—extra.

$1095*
AND UP

P.S. The new LaSalle V-8 may be purchased on the G. M. Installment Plan with monthly payments to suit your purse.

1937
LASALLE SERIES 50

After three years with an Oldsmobile-based straight eight, LaSalle returned to Cadillac V-8 power in '37. Thanks to the reasonably priced Cadillac Series 60, LaSalle could build a inexpensive car based on Cadillac components. In fact, the '37 was the lowest-priced LaSalle ever sold. Buyers responded, and LaSalle had its best year ever with 32,000 produced—up from 13,000 in '36. LaSalle's wheelbase increased from 120 to 124 inches, and horsepower rose from 105 to 125. Styling was fresh but retained LaSalle's trademark narrow grille first seen on the '34 model. LaSalle would keep its distinctive grille to the end. Ralph DePalma, famous race car driver and winner of the 1915 Indianapolis 500, paced the 1937 Indy 500 in a LaSalle convertible coupe similar to the one pictured.

PRESENTING THE SENSATIONAL NEW

CADILLAC *Sixty* SPECIAL

THE NEWEST CAR IN THE WORLD

T HERE HAS NEVER BEEN another car like the *new* Cadillac Sixty Special . . . a car with such definite modernity of line, yet so obviously right in taste . . . a precedent-breaking car prophetic of motor cars not yet on other drawing boards, yet a car wholly devoid of freakish trappings.

THERE HAS NEVER BEEN anything like the vivid, spirited performance of this car . . . with its inexhaustible vitality, its eager-flow-

ing power, its quiet, obedient responsiveness! There has never been anything like its inviting, all-embracing comfort . . . davenport seats, with extra width and extra depth. There has never been anything like the vision with which you drive the Cadillac Sixty Special . . . there is more outward vision than in any closed car ever built heretofore.

THERE ARE BOLD STROKES OF INSPIRED DESIGN in the Sixty Special. There are no running-

boards—you step right in, through doors of generous width. From every angle—the Cadillac Sixty Special is, beyond dispute, *the newest car in the world!*

IF YOU ARE TIRED OF THE COMMONPLACE —if you want the only really different car of the year—then by all means accept our invitation to drive this matchless Cadillac Sixty Special. Its performance . . . in your own hands . . . will make the most extravagant description seem faint praise indeed!

There is also a new Cadillac Sixty in more conventional mold, and selling at a price we believe represents the greatest value in the motor car market. It differs from the Special in appearance and appointment—it is one with the Special in quality and in performance. And as to performance . . . the Cadillac Sixty is unquestionably America's finest-performing eight cylinder car! See it!

1938
SIXTY SPECIAL

With the V-16 Cadillac used engineering to gain a hold on the luxury market, while the Sixty Special established Cadillac's dominance in styling. The Sixty Special was one of the great designs of the Thirties and influenced car design for years afterward. The distinctive roof looked more like a convertible top than a Thirties sedan roof. The side windows were large with thin, elegant chrome frames instead of the normal thick, painted stampings. The effect was similar to that of a postwar hardtop. The Special was the first sedan with a fully integrated trunk. Previous sedan trunks were upright boxes grafted onto the rear of the car. The car was built on a double drop frame that made it three inches lower than other Cadillacs. The low build allowed the elimination of running boards.

1939
SIXTY SPECIAL

The Sixty Special was the first project of Bill Mitchell who would later head General Motors' design department in the Sixties and Seventies. It has been estimated that Mitchell determined the appearance of 72 million cars. The Sixty Special remained one of his favorite designs. For its second year, the Sixty Special got a new grille and was available with two-tone paint jobs. The Special was planned as a sport sedan with a low build and stiff frame for good handling. It was the first car from Detroit's Big Three without running boards. Power was provided by Cadillac's 346-cid 135-hp V-8 and was transmitted by a tough, quick-shifting three-speed gearbox that was later a favorite of hot-rodders. The $2090 sedan was priced between Cadillac's entry-level Series 61 and the big Series 75.

MORE POPULAR THAN ALL THE OTHERS COMBINED

ONE OF THE FIRMEST INDICATIONS of a return to normalcy in America is the renewed interest in products of quality. Once more, Americans are realizing that the *best* is the *truest value.*

Confirming this is the preference accorded Cadillac-Fleetwood. People who spend above $2,000 for their motor cars are making Cadillac their overwhelming choice. Actually, among all cars in this field, more Cadillacs are purchased than *all* others combined!

Chances are, however, that Cadillac's dominance of the fine-car field only serves to confirm your own judgment of

these distinguished cars. For you probably feel, instinctively, that a Cadillac-Fleetwood *should* excel in all that makes a fine car desirable.

But even though you expect these cars to represent the final achievement in beauty, in luxury, in safety and in performance . . . you will still be agreeably surprised when you ride in a *new* Cadillac-Fleetwood.

The time and experience of your Cadillac dealer are yours to command. Why not consult him today—and learn how richly this preference for Cadillac-Fleetwood is deserved?

CADILLAC FLEETWOOD V-8 *and* 16

1939
SERIES 75

The Series 75 Fleetwood 7-passenger Imperial sedan pictured cost $3360 and weighed 5025 lbs. It was powered by a 140-hp V-8. The center car in the ad is a V-16 and has a more prominent grille than Fleetwood V-8s. In 1938, Cadillac replaced its 452-cid overhead-valve V-16 with a 431-cid L-head V-16. The new engine was lighter and more compact, yet developed the same 185 hp. Cadillac sold the V-16 through 1940, even though it probably made a profit only in '30 and '31. The V-16 was Cadillac's bid to be the leading luxury car, and with General Motors' money they could stick with it. As late as 1937, Packard could claim that it sold half the luxury cars in America, but by '39 Cadillac could claim that it sold more cars costing more than $2000 than all its competitors combined.

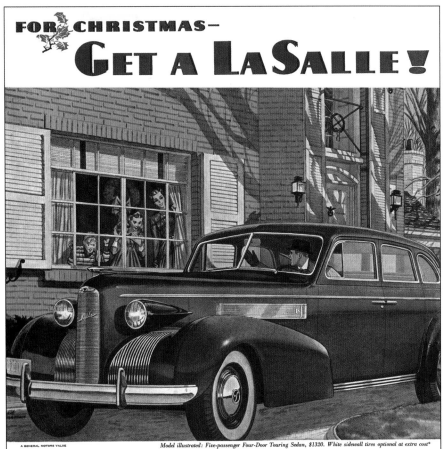

1939
LASALLE SERIES 50

The restyled LaSalle of '39 was four inches shorter. It shared body shells with Buick, Oldsmobile, and Pontiac. The body boasted a 25 percent increase in glass for a lighter appearance and better visibility. There had been complaints that the 1937–38 cars didn't offer a good view of the road. Following the trend started by Cadillac's Sixty Special, there were no running boards, though they could be added as an option. The polished wood and multiple round gauges of early Thirties dashboards had been replaced by painted metal and chrome radio speaker grilles as the Thirties came to a close. The opera coupe pictured was the least expensive body style at $1240. All LaSalles were powered by a 125-hp V-8. After a bad year in '38, sales jumped 41 percent to 22,000.

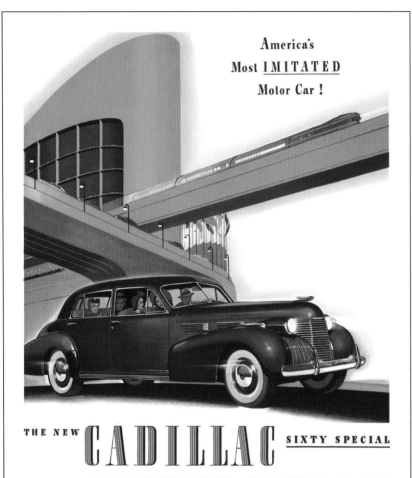

America's
Most **IMITATED**
Motor Car !

THE NEW **CADILLAC** **SIXTY SPECIAL**

Among the most enthusiastic owners of the Cadillac Sixty Special are scores of men who hold prominent positions in the automotive industry. ¶ So great is their preference for this dynamic beauty that we could safely call it the favored car of the men who are "in the know." ¶ In fact, the Sixty Special has been given the sincerest tribute the automotive industry knows how to bestow —the tribute of imitation. It is easily America's most imitated motor car. ¶ But regardless of efforts to duplicate its styling and performance, the Sixty Special stands uniquely alone. No other car approaches it for performance, comfort, vision, or handling ease. ¶ Borrow a Sixty Special from your Cadillac dealer and see for yourself. Whether you drive five minutes or five hours, you'll find it the sweetest-riding, sweetest-handling car you ever tried.

The Cadillac Motor Car Division builds LaSalle, Cadillac and Cadillac-Fleetwood cars. Prices begin at $1240. Illustrated is the Cadillac-Fleetwood Sixty Special, $2090, delivered at Detroit. Transportation based on rail rates, state and local taxes (if any), optional equipment—white sidewall tires and accessories—extra. Prices subject to change without notice.

Have you seen the new Sixty-Two—the lowest-priced Cadillac for 1940? Better take a look—it's a great car and a great value.

1940
SIXTY SPECIAL

The Sixty Special entered its third year with modest changes. The grille was bolder, and the trunk badge incorporated the Cadillac crest. The price remained $2090 for all three years. Sidemounted spare tires made their last appearance on Cadillacs in 1940. A popular option in the early Thirties, they didn't always go well with the streamlined cars of later years, although the Special wears them well. The metal spare tire cover not only made for a neat appearance, but it protected the tires from the sun, which some believed caused deterioration. An open-front town car version of the Sixty Special was added for 1940. The town car started at $3465 and sold only 15 copies. Divider window and sunroof were optional, but neither was popular. The sunroof tended to leak and was dropped after '41.

1940
LASALLE SERIES 52 SPECIAL

LaSalle was available in two series for 1940. The Series 50 (shown in the ad) was a carryover from '39, while the Series 52 Special (pictured) was new with a body shared with the Cadillac Series 62. The Special was lower, wider, and heavily influenced by the Cadillac Sixty Special. Many consider it the most beautiful LaSalle built. The 52 Special averaged more than $100 more than comparable base 50s, but it was the best-selling line. Production rose to more than 24,000, but '40 would be LaSalle's last year. LaSalle's niche was squeezed between expensive Buicks and entry-level Cadillacs. It had been long suspected that the prestige of the Cadillac name could sell more cars than LaSalle. The Cadillac Series 61 replaced LaSalle in '41, and 29,247 were sold.

1941
SERIES 62

With the V-16 gone, all Cadillacs used one engine. The 346-cid V-8 got a power boost to 150 hp from a higher compression ratio and other improvements. That was enough power to propel the lightest models 0-60 mph in about 15 seconds. General Motors' Hydra-Matic, the first fully automatic transmission, was introduced on Oldsmobiles in '40 and became a $100 option on Cadillacs in '41. Thirty percent of Cadillac buyers ordered automatics that first year. The broad eggcrate grille introduced in '41 has been a recurring Cadillac theme ever since. The hood ornament goddess was also new and served as a hood-release handle. The Series 62 convertible pictured cost $1645. The Series 61 took the place of the discontinued LaSalle, and the fastback coupe in the ad was the least expensive Cadillac at $1345.

The finest personal transportation in the world

AMONG ALL manufacturers of motor cars, Cadillac alone has maintained *one* standard. Cadillac has concentrated *exclusively* on the production of the best motor cars money can build or buy.

Portrayed above is the natural result—the finest personal transportation in the world.

The superiority of the Cadillac-Fleetwood is everywhere apparent. The very doors proclaim it—they are generously sized for *easy* entrance and exit. The luxurious interiors assert it even more emphatically—nowhere else will you find such roominess and comfort. And a ride provides the strongest evidence of all—for the engine is the most powerful Cadillac V-8 ever built.

There is an easy and enjoyable way to prove that a Cadillac-Fleetwood has no serious rival—*drive* one!

Cadillac *Fleetwood*

GENERAL MOTORS' FINEST CAR

1941
SERIES 75

The Series 75 had new but dignified styling for '41. With the disappearance of Series 75 coupes and convertibles after '40, all 75s were limousines or long-wheelbase sedans. The Series 75 dominated the American limousine market until Cadillac discontinued factory-built limos after 1987. The 75 was available with or without jump seats or divider window. A switch in the rear armrest controlled the divider. The car pictured has a divider window but no jump seats. Only 132 were so equipped out of almost 2000 Series 75s built. This car cost $3150 when new and weighed 4810 lbs. The 136-inch wheelbase allowed generous room in the rear compartment. As is traditional for limousines, the front compartment is upholstered in black leather while the rear is cloth.

1942
SERIES 61

The United States entered World War II on December 8, 1941, and Cadillac car production ended on February 4, 1942. No one knew when car production would resume, and this ad assures car buyers that a Cadillac will give years of reliable service until new cars are available again. Wartime gas rationing was also a concern, and Cadillac claimed 14-17 mpg from its efficient V-8. A pair of Cadillac V-8s, along with Hydra-Matic transmissions, powered M-5 and M-24 tanks during the war. The engines proved tough and reliable in war use. Even before the war started, Cadillac had been supplying precision parts to General Motors' Allison Engineering for use in aero engines that powered fighter planes. The Series 61 coupe pictured was Cadillac's least expensive car at $1450. The gas cap was concealed under a taillight assembly.

1947
SERIES 62

After a three-year gap because of World War II, Cadillac resumed car production in October '45. To get the assembly lines moving quickly as possible, the '42 models were put back in production with only minor changes. In 1947, Cadillac was still struggling to meet demand, and the sellers market would last for several more years. This ad states that a new Cadillac will be worth the wait. In postwar America, Cadillac was the new symbol of success. The Series 62 convertible pictured was perhaps the most desirable automobile in a car-hungry nation. There were still postwar shortages of materials, but Cadillac managed to build 61,926 cars in the '47 model year. Only 6755 were the $2902 convertible. The Series 62 sedan in the ad was more numerous with 25,834 built. It was priced at $2523.

1948
SERIES 61

The '48 Cadillacs had new postwar styling with the first tailfins. Tailfins were inspired by the verical stabilizers of the Lockheed P-38 Lightning fighter plane. At first tailfins were just small bumps on the rear fenders, but they would grow to great heights by the end of the Fifties. Fins not only became a long-standing Cadillac hallmark but were copied worldwide. At $2728, the Series 61 club coupe (pictured) was the least expensive model. Many consider it the prettiest American fastback. The dash grouped all the instruments in a pod. This was expensive to build and was dropped after one year. The venerable L-head V-8 made a final appearance in '48. The smooth-running engine had served Cadillac since 1936 and proved its toughness in tanks during WWII.

Jewels by Harry Winston

Cadillac

1949
DE VILLE

The 1949 Cadillacs were powered by a new overhead-valve V-8 that would influence American engine design for the next 30 years. The overhead-valve layout allowed higher compression ratios to take advantage of new high-octane fuels developed during the war. The 331-cid V-8 put out 160 hp, while the 346-cid L-head engine it replaced put out 10 fewer hp and was 200 lbs heavier. The new V-8 made Cadillac one of the fastest cars in America. The Coupe de Ville was one of the first production hardtop convertibles. The hardtop was similar to a convertible but had a non-folding metal roof instead of cloth top. It was a popular bodystyle into the Seventies. Starting in '49, Cadillac used expensive jewelry or women's clothing in its ads. This ad style would continue into the Sixties.

1950
SERIES 61

Cadillacs had new styling for 1950 and all coupes
were hardtops. Cadillac's least expensive car was the
Series 61 hardtop coupe pictured that cost $2761.
The Series 61 rode on a 122-inch wheelbase, while
the Series 62 sedan in the ad used a 126-inch chassis.
Although Cadillac was on its second restyling since
World War II and used an advanced overhead-valve
V-8, the chassis was a prewar design. The Cadillac
V-8 was a popular installation in Fifties performance
and racing cars. American sportsman Briggs Cunning-
ham raced two Cadillacs at the 1950 LeMans 24-hour
road race. One was a nearly stock Series 61 hardtop
coupe and the other a Cadillac chassis with special
racing body. The stock coupe finished 10th and the
special 11th out of a starting field of 60. A Cadillac-
powered Allard finished third.

Jewels by Laykin *Et Gir* at I. Magnin.

IT'S A WONDERFUL YEAR TO MAKE THE MOVE!

What a wonderful, wonderful year this is for a motorist to take possession of his first Cadillac car! For whoever discovers the joys of Cadillac ownership behind the wheel of this beautiful Golden Anniversary creation is in for a "once-in-a-lifetime" experience. He'll be introduced to Cadillac's luxury and comfort at a time when Cadillac has made its greatest interior advancements in over half a century. He'll learn the thrill of Cadillac's mag-

nificent performance at a time when many of Cadillac's finest engineering achievements have just made their appearance. And he'll first enjoy the *pride* of Cadillac ownership at a time when Cadillac's reputation and prestige are at an all-time high. So if you have been thinking of placing your order for a Cadillac—then come in and see us at your first opportunity. One mile behind the wheel will convince you—*it's a wonderful year to make the move!*

YOUR

Cadillac

DEALER

1952
SERIES 62

Cadillac celebrated its 50th anniversary in '52. The vee under the Cadillac crest changed from chrome to gold for the occasion. The 331-cid V-8 gained a four-barrel carburetter and other improvements that raised horsepower to 190. A new rear bumper contained outlets for the dual exhaust pipes. *Motor Trend* tested a '52 Cadillac and recorded a 109.6-mph top speed. Hydra-Matic 4-speed automatic transmission became standard on all Cadillacs except the big Series 75 limousines. Power steering was a new $198.43 option for Cadillacs. The entry level Series 61 had been dropped during 1951. Though Cadillac's volume needed a low-priced model before World War II, with postwar prosperity the Series 61 was no longer needed. The Series 62 convertible cost $4163, and 6400 were built.

1953
FLEETWOOD SIXTY SPECIAL

Cadillac ads often stressed practicality and economy. Although that seemed unlikely for a luxury car, it was true. The make's resale values were so high in the early Fifties that, at trade-in time, Cadillac owners got most of their original purchase price back. Cadillac's advanced V-8 delivered unusually good fuel economy for a big luxury car. Even though horsepower rose to 210 in '53, fuel economy actually improved. Positioned between the volume Series 62 and the Series 75 limousine was the Series Sixty Special. Mounted on its unique 130-inch wheelbase, it was Cadillac's largest "owner-driven" car. It had a more luxurious interior and more standard equipment than the Series 62. During the first half of the Fifties, Specials were identified by a row of vertical chrome louvers on the rear portion of the car. Cadillac built 20,000 of the $4305 sedans. A Sixty Special weighed 4415 lbs.

1953
DE VILLE

Cadillac's Coupe de Ville hardtop continued to gain in popularity. For four years straight, the more expensive de Ville outsold the Series 62 coupe. The de Ville had plusher interior trim and cost $3995 versus $3571 for the Series 62. Cadillac built 14,550 de Villes for the model year. Cadillacs were getting flashier. The 50th anniversary golden vee trim from '52 was retained, and gold spread to other trim also. Styling chief Harley Earl hated the extended use of gold, but it was popular with customers and dealers. He had little choice but to grudgingly comply. Chrome wire wheels were a new option in '53. Cadillac's bomb-shaped bumper guards got bigger as the Fifties progressed. Cadillac's glamorous Eldorado convertible debuted in '53. Only 532 of the $7750 cars were built, but the Eldorado name would be in Cadillac's lineup for almost 50 years.

The fortunate woman who enjoys possession of a 1954 Cadillac would find it difficult, indeed, to single out the one quality of the car which she finds most rewarding. Cadillac's new performance, for instance, is a constant joy through every mile . . . its great beauty is a source of unending pride and satisfaction . . . its marvelous luxury delights her every time she glances about the car's interior . . . and its remarkable economy is a continuing compliment to her practical wisdom. For, truly, this magnificent motoring creation is superlative in *every* respect. If you have not as yet discovered this for yourself, you should visit your Cadillac dealer without delay. You'll be welcome at any time.

* * *

Dress designed by Hattie Carnegie expressly for the Cadillac Convertible.

Cadillac

CADILLAC MOTOR CAR DIVISION • GENERAL MOTORS CORPORATION

1954
SERIES 62

The restyled '54 Cadillacs were longer, lower, and wider than the previous models. The wraparound windshield appeared on the '53 Eldorado and spread to all other Cadillac models in '54. Within a few years, almost every American car had a wraparound windshield. Power steering became standard on all Cadillacs while power bakes were optional. The V-8's power rose from 210 to 230 hp. The Series 62 was the smallest Cadillac line, but it used a long 129-inch wheelbase—up three inches from the previous year. The extra length benefited rear seat legroom. The Series 62 sedan pictured was the most popular model with 34,252 built. It cost $3933 and weighed 4370 lbs. The Series 62 convertible in the ad cost $4404 and weighed 4610 lbs. Cadillac built 6310.

GOWN DESIGNED BY PIERRE BALMAIN EXPRESSLY FOR THE CADILLAC SERIES SIXTY SPECIAL

There are few occasions in a woman's life as gratifying as the arrival of her family's first Cadillac car. Its inspiring beauty, for instance, becomes a source of great pride and pleasure. Its marvelous performance and handling ease introduce her to a new measure of motoring enjoyment. And its extraordinary comfort and safety add to the contentment and peace of mind of every family journey. Of course, the woman who welcomes a new Cadillac into the family in 1955 will be more richly rewarded than ever before—in *all* of these regards. For the car is now far finer in every way—and offers more of everything to make her proud and happy. Why not visit your dealer soon—and see for yourself? You'll be welcome at any time!

Jewelry · Van Cleef and Arpels

Cadillac

CADILLAC MOTOR CAR DIVISION · GENERAL MOTORS CORPORATION

1955
FLEETWOOD SIXTY SPECIAL

Once again the Sixty Special was sized between the base Series 62 and the Series 75 limos. The Sixty Special was four inches longer than the 62 with a 133-inch wheelbase. The Sixty had standard power windows and front seat. Air conditioning was a $620 option. Early air conditioners were bulky, and some of the components were in the trunk. The air intakes at the base of the rear roof pillars were for the air conditioning unit. Plexiglass tubes ran from the rear parcel shelf to the headliner where vents distributed cool air to the passengers. The pod to the left of the steering wheel is the optional Autronic Eye, an automatic headlight dimmer. Many of the Fifties Cadillac ads were aimed at women—either to buy a Cadillac of their own or in this case to influence "the arrival of her family's first Cadillac car."

"Guests of Honor" Wherever They Go!

Not long after a motorist takes delivery of his first Cadillac car, he makes a truly wonderful and thrilling discovery.

No matter where he travels at the wheel of his Cadillac, he finds that he is accorded an *extra* measure of courtesy and respect.

And this discovery will be all the more reward-ing for the man or woman who makes the move to Cadillac in 1955. For the "car of cars" now offers more of everything to inspire the respect and admiration of people everywhere.

Its world-famous beauty, for example, is more majestic and distinctive than ever before. Its cele-brated interior luxury and elegance are far more

wonderful to behold . . . and to enjoy. And its performance is, from every standpoint, the finest in Cadillac history!

If you haven't as yet taken the time for a per-sonal inspection and demonstration of the 1955 Cadillac—you ought to come in soon and do so.

You'll be a most welcome guest—at any time!

YOUR CADILLAC DEALER

1955
SERIES 62

The Series 62 hardtop coupe pictured and Coupe de Ville shown in the ad were externally identical except for the De Ville's small "Coupe de Ville" script under the rear quarter window. The De Ville had fancier up-holstery with multiple tufts, while the 62's interior was simpler—and, to modern eyes, perhaps more elegant. The Series 62 coupe was the least expensive model at $3882, while the Coupe de Ville cost $4305. Cadil-lac raised the V-8's compression ratio to 9.00:1. That, together with other improvements, upped horsepower to 250. The Eldorado engine had twin four-barrel carburetors that increased horsepower to 270 and was optional on all other Cadillacs. The American economy was booming in '55, and Cadillac had record sales with 140,777 built for the model year.

1956
FLEETWOOD SIXTY SPECIAL

With the horsepower race intensifying, Cadillac increased the size of its overhead-valve V-8 from 331 cid to 365. It also increased the compression ratio to 9.75:1, which, in combination with the displacement increase, bumped horsepower to 285. Eldorados, with their twin four-barrel carburetors, saw horsepower increase to 305. The Eldo engine was optional on other models. A new Hydra-Matic automatic transmission shifted more smoothly than its predecessors, but Tom McCahill of *Mechanix Illustrated* suggested that "...it is sopping up a great deal more horsepower." Power brakes became standard equipment on all models. The Sixty Special cost $5047, and 17,000 were sold. Although auto industry sales were down slightly in '56, Cadillac's model year production rose to 154,577.

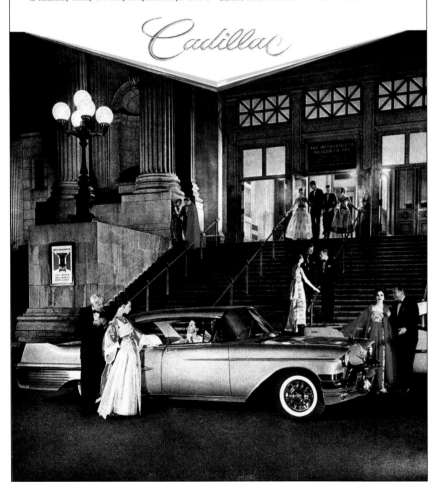

1957
FLEETWOOD SIXTY SPECIAL

Cadillacs had new styling and a new chassis for '57. Although it's hard to believe today, at the time customers and dealers complained that the new Cadillacs looked too small. The new frame consisted of two square-section steel tubes welded together to form a big X. The frame was stiffer and also allowed Cadillac to lower its cars by three inches. The new frame lacked side rails and, according to *Motor Trend,* "there was more vulnerability to damage in mid-ship collisions, despite strengthened rocker panels." The 365-cid V-8 had redesigned cylinder heads with higher 10.0:1 compression. Horsepower was 300 for all models, although an optional 325-hp engine with dual four-barrel carbs was available for Eldorado. The Sixty Special was offered only as a hardtop sedan.

This is the Eldorado Brougham—designed, styled and custom-crafted to create a new standard of automotive excellence. Now available in limited numbers, it is, in every way, the finest and most admired motor car ever to bear the Cadillac name.

CADILLAC MOTOR CAR DIVISION · GENERAL MOTORS CORPORATION

1958
ELDORADO BROUGHAM

Cadillac entered the ultra-luxury market with the Eldorado Brougham of 1957. At $13,074, it was almost three times as expensive as Cadillac's Series 62 coupe. Only 704 were built during two years of production. It was replaced by a second generation Brougham built in 1959–60. There were no options on Broughams. Standard equipment included air conditioning, power steering and brakes, power seat with memory, power windows and locks, cruise control, automatic headlight dimmer, digital clock, drink tumblers, vanity cases stocked with cosmetics, remote trunk release, air suspension, and alloy wheels. Upholstery was available in 44 choices of leather or wool broadcloth. The car was capped by a brushed stainless-steel roof. The 365-cid V-8 produced 325 hp in '57 and rose to 335 in '58 with the addition of triple two-barrel carburetors.

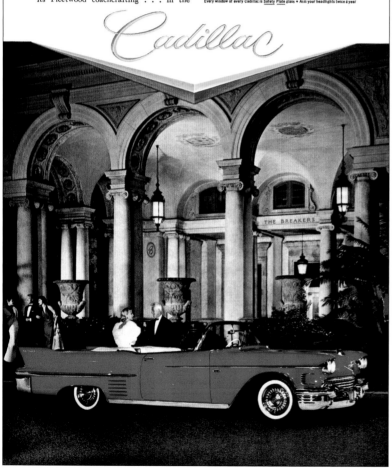

1958
SERIES 62

Fifties excess reached its peak in 1958. Cadillacs were big and had more chrome than ever. A sharp recession hurt sales of all but economical compact cars. Cadillac production dropped from 146,841 in '57 to 121,778. Americans were ready for smaller cars with less glitz. The failure of the Edsel was in part because of this shift. Cadillac raised its compression ratio again, and horsepower went up to 310 for the standard engine. Air suspension, introduced as standard equipment on the '57 Eldorado Brougham, was a $215 option on all other '58 Cadillacs. Air suspension gave a smooth ride but tended to leak. Quad headlights were another feature from the '57 Brougham that spread to the rest of the Cadillac line. Cadillacs of this period often hid the fuel filler under the taillights and the exhaust outlets in the rear bumper. The Series 62 convertible cost $5454.

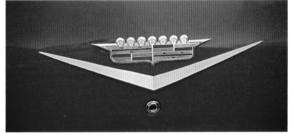

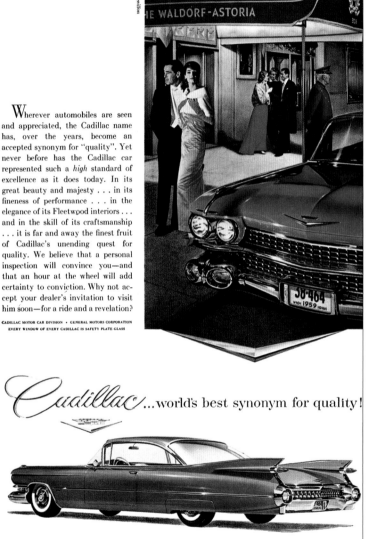

1959
SERIES 62

The '59 Cadillac convertible was a Fifties icon. Tailfins soared to their tallest height. Cadillac designers were enamored with aircraft, and the jet influence can be seen in the twin taillight design. The back-up light pods in the rear bumper resemble the exhaust ports of a jet. Up front, the grille was composed of chrome knobs. That grille pattern was repeated in the rear bumper. Yet for all the exuberance of the grille and tail design, the flanks of the car were clean and sweeping. That combination produced an American classic. The Series 62 convertible pictured cost $5455 and 11,130 were built, while the similar Series 62 hardtop coupe shown in the ad cost $4892 with 21,947 built. The hardtop's roof was supported by thin pillars that gave the impression of openness.

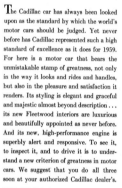

The Cadillac car has always been looked upon as the standard by which the world's motor cars should be judged. Yet never before has Cadillac represented such a high standard of excellence as it does for 1959. For here is a motor car that bears the unmistakable stamp of greatness, not only in the way it looks and rides and handles, but also in the pleasure and satisfaction it renders. Its styling is elegant and graceful and majestic almost beyond description . . . its new Fleetwood interiors are luxurious and beautifully appointed as never before. And its new, high-performance engine is superbly alert and responsive. To see it, to inspect it, and to drive it is to understand a new criterion of greatness in motor cars. We suggest that you do all three soon at your authorized Cadillac dealer's.

CADILLAC MOTOR CAR DIVISION • GENERAL MOTORS CORPORATION
EVERY WINDOW OF EVERY CADILLAC IS SAFETY PLATE GLASS

Cadillac . . . the new measurement of greatness

1959
SERIES 62

Everyone talks about the '59 Cadillacs' styling and towering tailfins, but they were also good cars that combined performance and comfort. Cadillac's V-8 was enlarged from 365-cid to 390 for '59, and horspower rose to 325. The big cars could go 0–60 mph in just 10.3 seconds, yet cruising with windows rolled up, the interior was hushed. Cadillac's X-frame allowed for a lower body that improved handling. The massive frame was also exceptionally strong and allowed Cadillac to build hardtops with thin roof pillars. Without that rigid frame, those bodies would have twisted apart. The 130-inch wheelbase provided a smooth ride and the generous interior room expected of a luxury car. The Series 62 hardtop sedan pictured cost $5080. The $5498 Sedan de Ville in the ad was externally identical except for the Sedan de Ville script on the rear fender. De Villes had a richer interior.

Boca Raton Hotel and Club is the place, Cadillac Sixty-Two Convertible is the car, elegant is the word.

THERE'S NOTHING LIKE A NEW CAR

Nothing else offers your family so much in so many ways as a new car. That's the case with any make, though we believe you'll find special rewards in one of our fine, new General Motors cars.

Don't dream—drive! That's what a new car seems to urge. Put your travel folder away and get out your suitcases. And what better way to travel than the make-your-own-schedule way in a brand-new car? You won't be on the road long before you realize again that nothing for the money can offer so much to the whole family in comfort, convenience, pleasure and safety as a new car. Any new car—though we believe you'll find more satisfaction in one of our eye-catching 1960 General Motors cars.

What a selection you have! Sizes from the Cadillac to the Corvair by Chevrolet; models from sleek sedans to snappy convertibles. There's one, beautifully made and advance-engineered, that's sure to fit your family perfectly.

Visit your GM dealer soon. You'll sit a little taller with your shoulders a little straighter in a new car. And you'll stay that way for many days to come, whether you're driving just around town or clear across the country.

GENERAL MOTORS
GO GM FOR '60

CHEVROLET · PONTIAC · OLDSMOBILE
BUICK · CADILLAC

All with Body by Fisher

FOR FAMILIES WHO'D RATHER DO THAN DREAM

1960
ELDORADO

Cadillac clipped its tailfins as the company toned down the excess of the Fifties. Fins were not only lower but a discreet, thin strip of red replaced the twin cone taillights of the '59s. The Series 62 convertible in the ad cost $5455 and sold 14,000 copies. The Eldorado Biarritz convertible pictured cost $7401 and only 1285 were sold. The Eldorado had a standard 345-hp V-8 with triple two-barrel carburetors. The Series 62 was powered by a 325-hp engine with a single four-barrel carb, but the Eldorado engine was optional. Since its introduction in 1953, the Eldorado convertible had been better trimmed with more standard equipment than the base convertible. Eldorado exterior styling was more distinct in some years than others. In 1960, it was only the chrome side trim that set Eldo apart.

The Sixty-Two Coupe • French embroidery on velvet from the Brooklyn Museum • Jeweled "V" and Crest created by Van Cleef and Arpels

A new Cadillac car is one of the few material possessions for which there is no completely acceptable substitute.

CADILLAC MOTOR CAR DIVISION, GENERAL MOTORS CORPORATION

1961
DE VILLE

Cadillac had new styling for '61. Tailfins were once again lower and complemented by skegs—long pointy fins along the bottom of the rear fenders. The "panoramic" wraparound windshield of the late Fifties was replaced by a conventional windshield, but with a little switchback at the bottom of the pillar. The cars had a lighter look than preceding years. Mechanically, Cadillacs were virtually unchanged under their new bodies. The 325-hp V-8 continued, but the 345-hp Eldorado engine was gone. The Series 62 hardtop coupe in the ad was the least expensive model at $4892. That price did not include heater or radio. Standard features we take for granted today were often optional in the Sixties—even on luxury cars. The $5252 Coupe de Ville pictured had a plusher interior and more standard equipment.

The Coupe de Ville · Jeweled "V" and Crest created in sapphires and diamonds by Cartier

Cadillac acclaim

It has been estimated that more than forty million motorists
would rather own a Cadillac than any other car.

Cadillac Motor Car Division · General Motors Corporation

1962
SERIES 62

Cadillacs were little changed for '62. Tailfins were once again lower, and the grille was revised. Cadillac pioneered clear-lens taillights that turned red when they lit up. Rear roof pillars were wider for a more formal look. Radios and heaters were finally standard equipment on all Cadillacs. Air conditioning was still optional, and 59 percent of Cadillac buyers ordered it. Cadillac's brochure advised customers that air conditioning "...is a prominent factor in maintaining value..."—meaning that cars without air were worth less at trade-in time. The $5385 Coupe de Ville in the ad had standard power windows and front seat. The Series 62 hardtop sedan lacked those power accessories and cost $5213. Cadillac set a new record with 160,840 cars built for the model year.

CADILLAC OWNERS DON'T ALWAYS AGREE *about why they bought the car. A great many report that unexcelled craftsmanship and quality led them to the "car of cars". Others say the size and solidity of the car, its silence and smoothness in motion, convinced them to make the move. Still another group state their selection stemmed from the confidence and pride they experience at the wheel of a Cadillac. The reasons are legion. But there is one subject upon which Cadillac owners unanimously agree: the new 1963 car is the most rewarding possession a man can have.*

Cadillac Motor Car Division • General Motors Corporation

1963
SERIES 62

Cadillacs were restyled for '63 with cleaner lines. Under the hood was a new V-8—the first redesign since 1949. The new engine had the same 390-cid displacement and 325-hp output of the old engine, but it was lighter and more compact. It also had the potential to grow to 500 cid, which it did in 1970. Cadillac sold 17,600 Series 62 convertibles. In the background of the ad is a Fleetwood Series 75, which was available with or without a divider window. The 75 rode on a 149.8-inch wheelbase, while all other models used a 129.5-inch wheelbase. The Series 75 would retain its Fifties-style wraparound windshield through '65. The limousine cost $9939 and weighed 5300 lbs. The Series 62 convertible shown in the ad and photos cost only $5590 and weighed 4545 lbs.

1964
DE VILLE

For '64, the V-8 was enlarged from 390-cid to 429, and horsepower rose to 340. De Villes used a new Turbo Hydra-Matic automatic transmission that replaced fluid coupling with a more efficient torque converter for better response. Cadillac could boast a top speed of 122 mph, 0–60 mph in 8.5 seconds, and the quarter mile in 16.8 seconds at 85 mph. Convenience wasn't neglected for performance. Comfort Control was the first fully automatic climate control, and Twilight Sentinel was the first automatic off/on headlight control. The base convertible moved from the Series 62 range to the De Ville family. The De Ville convertible pictured cost $5612. A premium Fleetwood Eldorado convertible was also available for $6630. The Coupe de Ville in the ad cost $5408.

1965
FLEETWOOD SIXTY SPECIAL

Cadillacs were restyled and re-engineered for '65.
Styling was clean and smooth. There was only a hint
of a tailfin in the rear fender. A new frame and revised
suspension improved ride and handling. The 340-
hp V-8 was unchanged from '64, but an improved
exhaust system made the cars quieter. The Fleetwood
sedans had a 133-inch wheelbase that was 3.5 inches
longer than Calais and De Ville. The Fleetwood also
had standard load-leveling suspension that compen-
sated for additional passengers or luggage. The car in
the ad has the optional $194 vinyl roof that makes it
a Fleetwood Brougham. A tilt and telescope steering
was a new option on all Cadillacs. Fleetwoods had a
laurel wreath instead of a vee with the Cadillac crest.
The Fleetwood Sixty Special cost $6479.

1966
DE VILLE

Cadillac convertible production reached its peak in '66 with 21,450—this included 19,200 De Villes and 2250 Eldorados. The De Ville convertible cost $5555 and had standard leather upholstery. A 129.5-inch wheelbase ensured plenty of room for both seats. All Cadillacs gained variable-ratio power steering that responded more quickly the farther the wheel was turned from center. A heated front seat was a new option. The Fleetwood 75 limousine (in the background of the ad) had all new styling and a new frame for '66. The low-volume 75 wasn't updated as often as the other Cadillac lines, but in '66 it caught up with the other models. The new body featured doors that wrapped into the roof for easier entry and exit. Its 149.8-inch wheelbase allowed three rows of seating.

1967
ELDORADO

The Eldorado coupe was a new kind of Cadillac. It was Cadillac's entry in the "personal car" market that included coupes such as Pontiac Grand Prix, Buick Riviera, and Ford Thunderbird. Eldorado was smaller than the other Cadillac models but, on a 120-inch wheelbase, it was still a big car. It was front-wheel drive at a time when the only other American front-drive car was its sister car, the Oldsmobile Toronado. Eldorado and Toronado were based on the same platform but differed in styling, engines, and suspension tuning. Eldorado used the same 340-hp V-8 as all the other Cadillacs. *Motor Trend* timed 0–60 in 8.9 seconds. Handling was better than large Cadillacs, but the ride was firmer than traditional Cadillac customers expected. The Eldorado cost $6277.

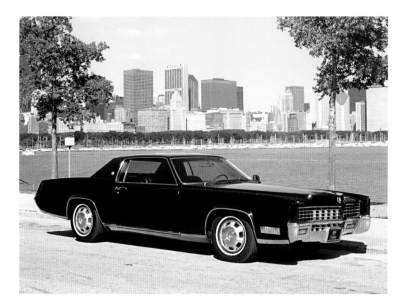

1968
DE VILLE

More accessories, new Federal emissions standards, and increasing weight were taxing the power of Cadillac's V-8. For '68, engine size was increased to 472 cid. Cadillac was able to boast of building the largest production engine in the world. Horsepower rose to 375 bhp, and torque was a mighty 525 pound-feet. Both De Ville coupe and convertible weighed 4600 lbs, yet the big V-8 could push them to a 120-mph top speed. For '68, hoods were stretched to the base of the windshields to conceal wipers. Power windows were standard on all Cadillacs. Air conditioning was still an option, but 96 percent of Cadillac buyers ordered it. Cadillac built almost 230,000 cars during the model year. Coupe de Villes (ad) accounted for 63,935, while 18,025 De Ville convertibles (photos) were sold.

1969 Coupe deVille. Cadillac Motor Car Division

Your first weekend with the beautiful new 1969 Cadillac will be an irresistible temptation to go traveling. With its brilliant new styling—and spirited performance to match—even the most familiar trip will take on new excitement.

Cadillac

1969
DE VILLE

Cadillac's styling was revised for '69. The parking lights and taillights wrapped into the sides to satisfy federal regulations for side marker lights. The front vent windows were eliminated for a neater appearance. General Motors introduced vent windows in 1933 as part of its No-Draft Ventilation, but improvements in forced-air ventilation and the popularity of air conditioning made vents unnecessary. The difference in price between the $5721 Coupe de Ville (ad) and the $5905 De Ville convertible (photos) was only $184, or 3 percent. Today's unibody construction makes convertible production more difficult, and the price premium for a convertible is often around 25 percent. Cadillac's convertible production dropped to 16,445 as the open-car market went into a rapid decline. The wheels on the car pictured are from a later model.

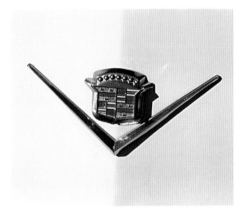

Eldorado Convertible. In all the world there's but one car to equal it.

In many ways, the all-new 1971 Fleetwood Eldorado Convertible by Cadillac is unique.

As the only luxury convertible now built in America, it is both dramatically beautiful and remarkably responsive. Young. Glamorous. Every inch an Eldorado—from its jewel-like standup crest to its beveled rear deck. It is truly one of the world's two most elegant personal cars.

Slide behind the wheel, and you quickly become aware that this is like no other convertible you've ever seen. The richness of the soft, pliable Sierra grain leather upholstery is available in a total of ten colors. The newly designed steering wheel sounds the horn when pushed anywhere in the padded center area. The gracefully curved instrument panel allows you to see all the gauges at a glance.

Turn the key, and you quickly become aware that this is like no convertible you've ever driven. Its 8.2 litre V-8 is the world's largest production passenger car engine. Yet it runs efficiently on no-lead and low-lead gas to reduce exhaust pollutants. You'll feel the difference made by front-wheel drive, variable-ratio power steering, power front disc brakes and Automatic Level Control.

It even converts uniquely. An ingenious new inward-folding Hideaway Top folds behind the seat when it is lowered. The results are a more graceful top-down appearance and full-width room for rear-seat passengers.

"And what other car," you might ask, "has credentials to match these?"

Only one. The magnificent new Eldorado Coupe by Cadillac.

According to its owners, it is the equal of the Eldorado Convertible. They point to its long, low distinctive design. Its luxuriously appointed interior. And its new coach windows—an Eldorado exclusive that accentuates its classic, personal car appearance.

The Eldorado Coupe. It, too, has the smoother, softer, quieter ride that results from Eldorado's new, longer wheelbase and new suspension. It, too, has side-guard beams in the doors for your added security. It, too, has all other Cadillac safety items—including easy-to-use seat and shoulder belts. It, too, offers a wide range of options for your driving ease and comfort.

A case in point is Cadillac's Twilight Sentinel. It turns driving lights on and off automatically in response to light conditions. It also allows you to leave headlamps and either cornering lamp on for up to 90 seconds to light your path from the car.

So it seems to come down to this: The only car you can compare to an Eldorado is another Eldorado. The Eldorado Convertible and Eldorado Coupe. No other automobiles anywhere are their equal.

Your Cadillac dealer cordially invites you to experience the singular pleasure of driving either of the world's most elegant personal cars. Or both.

Cadillac Motor Car Division

Cadillac

1971
ELDORADO

The front-wheel-drive Eldorado had its first redesign since its 1967 introduction. The car looked bigger, even though it was only .6-inch longer overall and 45 lbs heavier. The suspension was softened for a better ride at the expense of handling. Power was provided by a 500-cid (or 8.2-liter) V-8 that developed 365 hp. All General Motors engines had lower compression in '71, allowing them to run on no-lead or low-lead regular gas for lower emissions. The Eldo coupe gained a convertible companion, while Cadillac dropped the De Ville convertible for '71. Eldorado was the only luxury convertible built in America. Eldorados had two features that were much copied during the Seventies. Both Eldos had a spring-loaded hood ornament, and the coupes reintroduced prewar coach windows. The convertible cost $7751. A three-month strike hampered production, and only 6800 convertibles were built.

Do people own Cadillacs because they get more out of life, or...

do people get more out of life because they own Cadillacs? It's hard to say. Because Cadillacs have been such an integral part of the good life for 70 years now. In prestige, in performance, in pure driving pleasure, probably nothing offers more deep-seated satisfaction than owning a Cadillac. Perhaps no other automobile receives such universal admiration and respect. Or can contribute more to your driving peace of mind. Small wonder then that Cadillac resale value is traditionally the highest of any car built in the land. The only question remaining is: Do you visit your authorized Cadillac dealer today...or tomorrow?

MARK OF EXCELLENCE

There's no question about this. Real progress is being made by Cadillac and others in the massive effort to remove the automobile from the air pollution problem. You can help by using no-lead or low-lead fuels. Getting a tune-up regularly. Having the emission control systems on your car checked often. Thank you. Cadillac Motor Car Division.

Cadillac

1972
DE VILLE

The Cadillac Coupe de Ville had a 130-inch wheelbase and was 225.8 inches long. This generation was the last of the giants. A downsized, but still big, De Ville debuted in '77. All Cadillacs were restyled for '71 and received only minor alterations for '72. A small but welcome change was the return of the vee under the Cadillac crest. A tradition since '46, the vee was removed from De Ville and Calais in '70—much to the chagrin of traditional Cadillac customers. In '72, all domestic automakers switched from gross horsepower ratings to more realistic net ratings. The 472-cid V-8's horsepower dropped from 345 to 220. This was an "on paper" change that had no effect on performance. *Motor Trend* accelerated a '71 Sedan de Ville 0–60 mph in 10.1 seconds. The '72 would have had similar performance.

Eldorado.

Life is too short to put it off for long.

Maybe for you, it was love at first sight. Eldorado can do that to people.

Or perhaps it's the way Eldorado owners talk about the car. The way it handles—with its renowned front-wheel drive, variable-ratio power steering and Automatic Level Control. The way it moves—with that exclusive Eldorado engine. The way it rides—smoother than ever in '74.

Or maybe you're looking for a luxury car that is basically different from the rest—a difference that goes beyond styling. Like the difference front-wheel drive makes in traction and stability.

Or it could just be that for you Eldorado is America's finest personal luxury car. And you're a person unaccustomed to second best.

There are many luxury cars.

But there is only one Eldorado.

And there's only one way to stop wanting it. That, of course, is to start enjoying it. The classic Coupe or America's only luxury Convertible.

Eldorado is but one of nine superb Cadillac models for 1974. So see your authorized Cadillac dealer about owning or leasing the Cadillac of your choice.

We suggest you do it soon. Life is just too short to put it off for long.

Cadillac
America's Number One Luxury Car.

1974
ELDORADO

The Oil Embargo of late 1973 had repercussions that would change the future of Cadillac. Cadillac had been the undisputed king of the American luxury car market since at least the end of World War II, but the market was changing. Higher fuel prices meant that luxury cars would have to be smaller and more frugal. The European competition was already compact and had better handling. They also had better fit and finish than Cadillacs of the Seventies. Cadillac was planning changes but in '74 still offered the kind of big cars that most Americans aspired to own. Eldorado's styling had been revised in '73. The biggest change was the addition of large, impact-absorbing bumpers that were required by federal regulations. The interior was freshened with a new dashboard and cushions on the doors that Cadillac referred to as the "soft-pillow" effect.

Last of a magnificent breed.

The Eldorado Convertible. Today an extraordinary luxury car...with front-wheel drive and four-wheel disc brakes. Tomorrow a classic. For this is more than one of the finest convertibles ever built.

It is the only convertible now built in America. And it will be our last. The very last. Because the Eldorado Convertible will not be offered in 1977. We suggest you visit your Cadillac dealer soon. Very soon.

1976
ELDORADO

By '76, Eldorado was the last convertible built in America, and Cadillac decided to send it off in a blaze of glory. The final 200 built were white commemorative editions, and TV cameras rolled as the last convertible slipped off the line. Fourteen-thousand convertibles were built for the '76 model year, but many more could have been sold. Speculators quickly bid prices well above the suggested $11,049 sticker. Prices went still higher at auctions, then reason set in and values crashed. The death of the convertible was exaggerated. Chrysler was the first to return to the convertible market in '82, and Cadillac followed in '84. Eldorado styling was freshened in '75 with skirtless rear fenders. In '76, four-wheel disc brakes were standard and hubcap centers were painted black.

A promise kept.

When Seville was first introduced, it was to be a new kind of American luxury car. International in size. Cadillac in craftsmanship. Timeless in styling. Some wondered. Seville has kept its promise. With subtle refinements to enhance its original concept. Because of our ongoing quest for perfection, Seville is even more desirable today ... one of the finest production cars built anywhere in the world. Your Cadillac dealer invites you to experience Seville. It's the only way.

Seville BY CADILLAC

1978
SEVILLE

Introduced in 1975, the Seville was 27 inches shorter, eight inches narrower, and nearly 1000 lbs lighter than a Sedan de Ville. Smaller did not mean cheaper. Seville was Cadillac's most expensive car short of the Series 75 limousine. Seville was built to fight the luxury imports, and Cadillac didn't cut corners on engineering or standard equipment. Cadillac also put great care in the assembly and finish of Seville. Most magazine road tests agreed Seville didn't handle as well as its European competitors, although it did handle better than most American cars. No one criticized its smooth, quiet ride. The 350-cid V-8 used electronic fuel injection for a good balance of power and economy. Built during the height of the CB craze, the car pictured has a factory-installed citizens band radio.